Totally into Fishing and Hunting

Big Game Hunting

Abby Badach Doyle

Gareth Stevens Publishing

Please visit our website, www.garethstevens.com. For a free color catalog of all our high-quality books, call toll free 1-800-542-2595 or fax 1-877-542-2596.

Library of Congress Cataloging-in-Publication Data

Names: Doyle, Abby Badach, author.
Title: Big game hunting / Abby Badach Doyle.
Description: New York : Gareth Stevens Publishing, [2023] | Series: Totally into fishing and hunting | Includes index.
Identifiers: LCCN 2022001361 (print) | LCCN 2022001362 (ebook) | ISBN 9781538279960 (set) | ISBN 9781538279977 (library binding) | ISBN 9781538279953 (paperback) | ISBN 9781538279984 (ebook)
Subjects: LCSH: Big game hunting–Juvenile literature.
Classification: LCC SK35.5 .D69 2023 (print) | LCC SK35.5 (ebook) | DDC 799.2/6–dc23/eng/20220120
LC record available at https://lccn.loc.gov/2022001361
LC ebook record available at https://lccn.loc.gov/2022001362

Portions of this work were originally authored by Andrew Law and published as *We're Going Big-Game Hunting*. All new material in this edition is authored by Abby Badach Doyle.

Published in 2023 by
Gareth Stevens Publishing
29 East 21st Street
New York, NY 10010

Editor: Abby Badach Doyle
Designer: Michael Flynn

Photo credits: Cover, p. 1 David Osborn/Shutterstock.com; series background (flag) BestGraphicsChoice/Shutterstock.com; p. 5 awon Shah/Shutterstock.com; p. 7 William T Smith/Shutterstock.com; p. 9 https://commons.wikimedia.org/wiki/File:Col._Roosevelt_with_his_big_bull_rhino_LCCN2010645479.jpg; p. 10 mmpixel91/Shutterstock.com; p. 11 IPK Photography/Shutterstock.com; p. 13 Roman Kosolapov/Shutterstock.com; p. 14 Kyle T Perry/Shutterstock.com; p. 15 PRESSLAB/Shutterstock.com; p. 16 Guy J. Sagi/Shutterstock.com; p. 17 SolidMaks/Shutterstock.com; p. 19 Sergey Shubin/Shutterstock.com; p. 21 Petr Salinger/Shutterstock.com; p. 23 milart/Shutterstock.com; pp. 24, 25 melissamn/Shutterstock.com; p. 27 nyker/Shutterstock.com; p. 28 cookedphotos/iStock; p. 29 FXQuadro/Shutterstock.com.

Printed in the United States of America

A NOTE TO READERS
Always talk with a parent or teacher before proceeding with any of the activities found in this book. Some activities require adult supervision.

A NOTE TO PARENTS AND TEACHERS
This book was written to be informative and entertaining. Some of the activities in this book require adult supervision. Please talk with your child or student before allowing them to proceed with any hunting activities. The author and publisher specifically disclaim any liability for injury or damages that may result from use of information in this book.

Some of the images in this book illustrate individuals who are models. The depictions do not imply actual situations or events.

CPSIA compliance information: Batch #CSGS23: For further information contact Gareth Stevens, New York, New York at 1-800-542-2595.

CONTENTS

WORDS IN THE GLOSSARY APPEAR IN BOLD TYPE THE FIRST TIME THEY ARE USED IN THE TEXT.

ON THE HUNT

Before grocery stores and **restaurants**, people needed to hunt for survival. That's still true in some parts of the world. A large animal, such as a bison, can feed many people.

Hunting can provide meat to eat, but it is also a social event. For many people, big game hunting is a family **tradition**. You get to spend time outdoors and learn important skills passed down over time. Today, big game hunting is a popular sport that millions of people enjoy.

KNOW THE FACTS!

In earlier times, the Lakota people hunted bison and used every part to survive. Hair was used to make rope. Skin became clothing and blankets. Bones were used to make arrows and tools.

Many big game hunters mount their best kills for display and to honor the animals' lives.

HOW BIG?

So, what is "big game?" In general, this term means large, wild animals that are hunted for sport. In the United States, big game refers to wild animals weighing 40 pounds (18.1 kg) or more. Each state has its own list of animals you are allowed to hunt.

Members of the deer family, such as white-tailed deer and mule deer, are considered big game. Moose, elk, wild boar, and bighorn sheep are all big game animals too. Predators like bears, cougars, and wolves are also considered big game.

KNOW THE FACTS!

Want to hunt a **swamp** monster? Go alligator hunting! Florida is the most popular state for that. You can also hunt alligators in the southeastern states of Texas, Louisiana, Georgia, and Mississippi.

The white-tailed deer is the most hunted big game animal in the United States.

HEALTHY POPULATIONS

In the past, some big game animals were hunted so much that they went **extinct**. These days, the United States has laws to protect wildlife. In other parts of the world, big game animals such as tigers and elephants are **endangered** because hunters disobey the laws.

Scientists closely study animal populations. Their findings are used to decide how many animals can safely be hunted in an area each season. If a population is too large, more hunting may be allowed.

KNOW THE FACTS!

In the 1800s, bison were nearly hunted to extinction. Once numbering in the millions, only a few hundred remained. Today, many bison populations are healthy. You can hunt bison in some states, including Wyoming, South Dakota, and Alaska.

President Theodore Roosevelt enjoyed hunting big game. He also helped make laws to protect wildlife.

WHEN TO GO

You can only hunt certain big game animals at certain times of the year. This time frame is called "open season" and is different for each animal and state. The fall months are usually the most popular for big game hunting.

Hunting can also be limited to certain times of day. These rules, and other hunting rules you'll learn in this book, are set by your state's fish and wildlife agency, or government department. Check with your local agency to learn open seasons in your state.

RULES AND SAFETY

Before you hunt big game, you will need to take a safety course. Hunting safety courses are offered online or in person. You also may need a hunting license.

A license is an official piece of paper to prove that you're a legal, or lawful, hunter in your state. States have different rules for how old you need to be to get a hunting license. Most states don't allow kids to hunt big game alone until they are 16 years old.

KNOW THE FACTS!

A hunting safety course will teach you how to safely shoot guns or bows. You will also learn other important things, like **responsible** handling of firearms, hunting laws, and first aid.

In many states, you can hunt at any age
with a licensed adult.

GEAR UP!

Many states require hunters to wear hunter orange or blaze orange. Many animals can't see this color, but to the human eye, it's very bright! Wearing orange will help other hunters see you and keep accidents from happening.

The color orange looks brown or gray to many big game animals.

Big game animals such as moose and elk are in season during chilly parts of the year. Wearing layers, or pieces of clothing over each other, will keep you warm. Wear gloves that allow your fingers to move and thick socks to keep your feet warm too.

HUNTING WITH RIFLES

Rifles are a popular firearm, or gun, used for big game hunting. Rifles are good at hitting targets that are far away. To hunt big game with a firearm, you'll need a rifle and the correct ammunition, or bullets.

KNOW THE FACTS!

Many big game hunters use scopes. A scope is a lens that lets a hunter see a faraway object close up. Using a scope makes it easier to aim and shoot a big game animal in the distance, or far away.

As a hunter, it's important to know your gun and use it safely. Make sure it's lawful. It's also best to avoid lead bullets, which are toxic to people and animals.

Smaller guns aren't used as much in big game hunting. With smaller bullets and shorter range, they're less likely to kill a large animal. It's better for animals to be killed cleanly than for them to be wounded and in pain.

HUNTING WITH BOWS

Bowhunting can be harder than using a rifle. It takes some time to set up and aim an arrow. You also have to get much closer to take your shot. When hunting big animals like elk, bear, or moose . . . that can be scary!

A compound bow uses cables and wheels that make it easier to pull back an arrow. Some states also permit crossbow hunting. Crossbows look like a combination of a gun and a bow and are very powerful.

KNOW THE FACTS!

Like bullets, arrows come in different sizes and weights. To hunt big game, you need a big, heavy arrow. You also need a bow string with a heavy draw weight to fire it.

One benefit of bowhunting is that you can reuse the arrows.

FOLLOW THE TRACKS

All big game hunters need to be good at tracking. Big game animals might not look fast because of their size, but they're quick. If they hear you, they'll most likely run. With practice, you'll get better at being quiet.

Bowhunters have a higher risk of not killing an animal instantly. Many animals will run away once they've been shot. It may take them a while to die. Hunters must follow an animal's trail, sometimes for several miles.

KNOW THE FACTS!

Animals are skilled at hiding in the **wilderness**. With practice,

Even a large animal, like this moose, can blend in with the trees.

SKILLS AND METHODS

Some hunters sit and wait in tree stands. Tree stands are tiny buildings or decks on trees to get a good view of an area. Other hunters **stalk** big game. This lets you cover more ground, but you have to be quiet!

You can also set up a trail camera. This helps hunters see what big game is in the area and pick a good hunting spot. Some cameras connect with wireless networks to send photos to your smartphone or computer.

KNOW THE FACTS!

Some hunters use special sprays or soaps to hide their scent from big game animals. You can also buy smelly things, like fake animal urine, or pee, to **attract** big game. It's gross, but it works!

Not all states allow trail cameras for big game hunting on public lands.

FIELD DRESSING AND TAGGING

After making a kill, the next step is field dressing. This is when you cool the animal's body by removing its **organs**. Do this right away so the meat doesn't spoil, or rot. You will need tools like a sharp knife, plastic gloves, a trash bag, and rope.

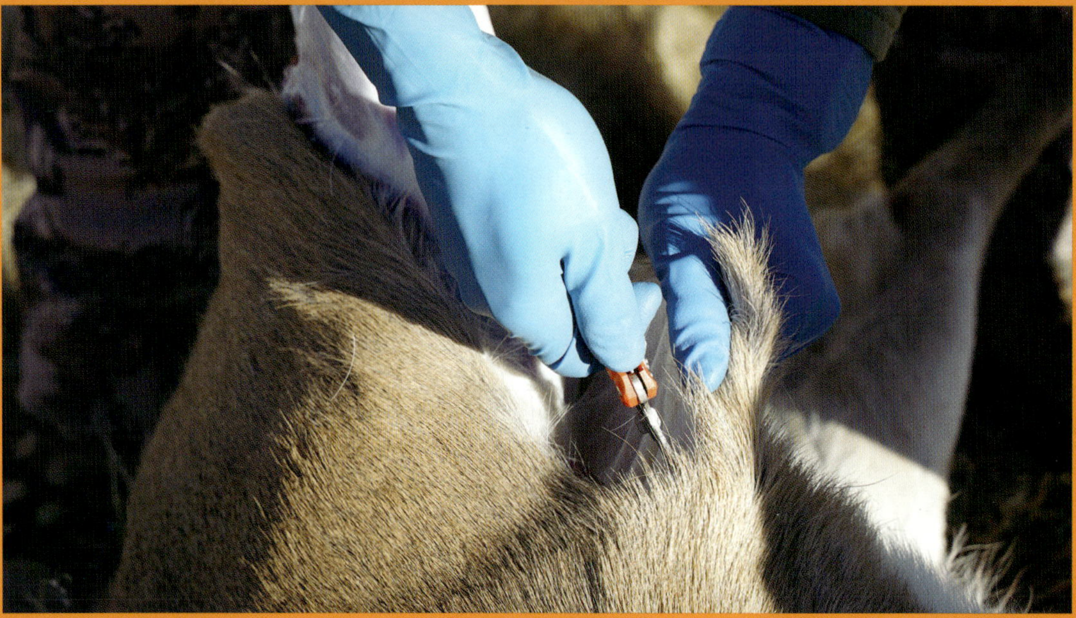

Big game animals are heavy. Make sure you have help to drag your kill!

The next step is to tag the animal. A tag is a form you add on to your hunting license. Your state's wildlife department uses tags to record information about the big game animals killed in a certain area.

Know the Facts!

Tags are handled differently by state. If **demand** is high to hunt a certain animal, the state might have a random drawing for tags to make it fair.

KEEPING IT FAIR

States have hunting laws to protect animal populations. Breaking a hunting law can mean an expensive fine or even the loss of your license. Breaking hunting laws on purpose is called poaching. Examples of poaching include killing more than your limit and hunting animals out of season.

Some people are not comfortable with the fact that big game animals are killed for sport. However, good hunters respect wildlife and care about nature. Money from hunting licenses, tags, and taxes goes to **conservation** efforts.

KNOW THE FACTS!

Big game trophy hunting in Africa is expensive, but legal. The "big five" animals are the lion, leopard, elephant, African buffalo, and rhinoceros. Hunting endangered animals is looked down on by conservationists.

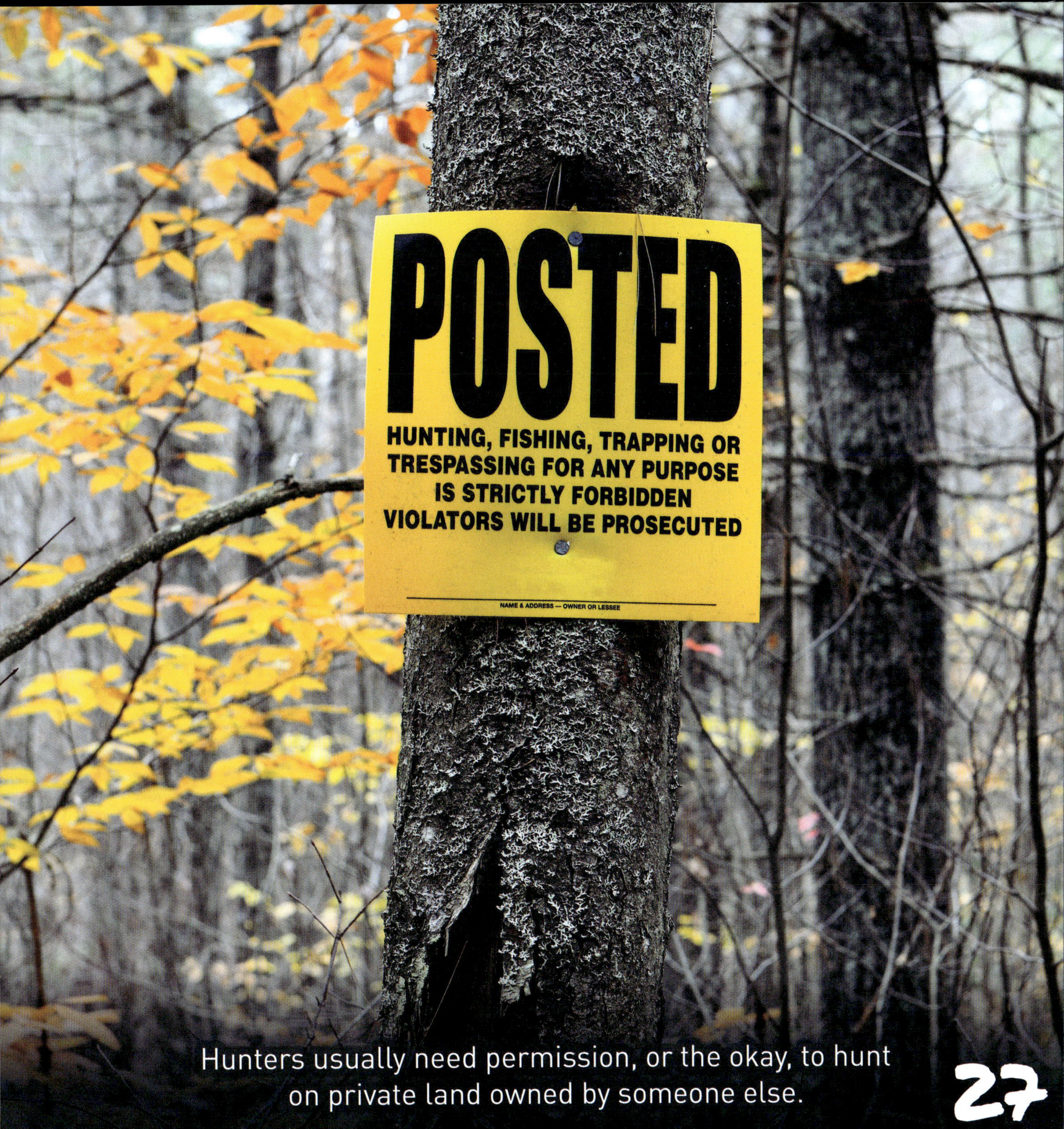

Hunters usually need permission, or the okay, to hunt on private land owned by someone else.

ENJOY THE HUNT

It's a big deal when you make a big kill! Many hunters enjoy having their picture taken with the animal they shot. Others make trophies, like mounts or rugs, from their animals.

KNOW THE FACTS!

Enjoying the meat can be one of the satisfying parts of hunting. Many people have favorite recipes for jerky, chili, stew, or burgers using big game meat.

Taxidermy is the art of making animal remains ready for display.

Hunting big game is not easy, but it can be very rewarding. Hunters travel to visit beautiful places and reconnect with the past. After all, people have been hunting for millions of years. Even if you don't make a kill, you will probably walk away with a wild story or two.

GLOSSARY

attract: to draw nearer

conservation: the care of the natural world. A conservationist is a person who works to prevent harm to animals, plants, or land.

demand: a strong need for something

endangered: in danger of dying out

extinct: when a certain species, or kind of animal, no longer exists

organ: a part inside an animal's body

responsible: able to be trusted to do what is right or to do the things that are expected or required

restaurant: a place where someone can buy and eat a meal

stalk: to follow an animal you are hunting by moving slowly and quietly

swamp: an area with trees that is covered with water at least part of the time

tradition: having to do with long-practiced customs

wilderness: a piece of uninhabited land left to grow wild

FOR MORE INFORMATION

BOOKS

Roe, Monica. *Elk Hunt Adventure*. Mankato, MN: Capstone, 2022.

Simons, Lisa M. Bolt. *Go Bowhunting!*. Mankato, MN: Capstone, 2021.

WEBSITES

Eddie Eagle Tree House
eddieeagle.com
The Eddie Eagle GunSafe® program from the National Rifle Association teaches kids important tips about gun safety.

Hunter-Ed
hunter-ed.com
View study guides and take state-approved hunting safety courses online.

Publisher's note to educators and parents: Our editors have carefully reviewed these websites to ensure that they are suitable for students. Many websites change frequently, however, and we cannot guarantee that a site's future contents will continue to meet our high standards of quality and educational value. Be advised that students should be closely supervised whenever they access the internet.

INDEX